# I Do think

# Love, Mercy and Holiness

SherAnne Shea Jubelirer

Published in the United States of America

ISBN 978-1-959173-82-3 (SC)
ISBN 978-1-959173-81-6 (HC)

**SherAnne Jubelirer Publishing**
222 West 6th Street
Suite 400, San Pedro, CA, 90731
ssjworkonly@gmail.com

Ordering Information and Rights Permission:

Quantity sales. Special discounts might be available on quantity purchases by corporations, associations, and others. For details, contact the publisher at the address above.

For Book Rights Adaptation and other Rights Permission. Call us at toll-free 1-888-945-8513 or send us an email at admin@stellarliterary.com.

# Contents


Forward ..................................................................................................... vi

Choosing Life And Wisdom Now ................................................................... 1

All that I do have to do that now ................................................................. 3

On Writings And That's Family ..................................................................... 4

We Need To Get A Way From Philly  And Over Around God Almighty ..................... 5

On Thought and Life Here ........................................................................... 7

On Doing The Holy Rosary With Love  Thru Blessed Mother, Mary Most Holy ......... 8

That's Mentalities That Had Hope ................................................................. 9

O For Thine Ever On Jesus! ....................................................................... 10

An Accolade ............................................................................................ 11

To Do That's Due ..................................................................................... 12

And Of Life and Of That's Love .................................................................. 13

We Were Even From The Holy Angels! ......................................................... 14

Seeking Jesus and  For a Circle of Loves And Graces ................................... 15

That's Before To Do A While, That's Us ....................................................... 16

Waking Up One Day .................................................................................. 17

Of That's Appreciation And  Of That's Gratitude ........................................... 19

Working With The Artist's Way Program Here ............................................... 20

Its Show Time and Starring ........................................................................ 21

On That's Love Forever! ............................................................................ 22

That's Tasks To Do ................................................................................... 23

As A Teacher, Maybe I Could Have Been ..................................................... 24

Of That's Works And Online  A perspective with God Almighty ........................ 26

Of To Do That's Faith And Graces .............................................................. 27

Good Days .............................................................................................. 28

An Experience Of  That's Love ................................................................... 29

A Poor City Neighborhood ......................................................................... 30

To Realize That Everyday Of Life Right Here ................................................ 31

A Drug Addict's Prayer in 1999 .................................................................. 32

Of Sufferings And Psychosis ...................................................................... 33

Jeff and Sherry in our beginnings of writings that was. ........................................ 34

To My Beloved ........................................................................................................ 35

Writer Do What Writers Do! .................................................................................. 36

Vanity Fair .............................................................................................................. 37

Of Often Taking Walks In Out In Lawndale ......................................................... 38

On Beauty To Do Here ........................................................................................... 39

Author Just needed or wanted more contact with others socially ......................... 40

Days of Believing The Lord Jesus Christ and To love Him So .............................. 41

History Of Love Of Good Fridays And Penance .................................................... 43

Doing And To Do Spiritual Disciplines in God Almighty ..................................... 44

Thinking And Dreaming Of God's Love ................................................................ 46

April 2010 Things Were Happening Of Then And Of Doing In Life ..................... 47

Growing And Learning and Living In the Same Way Since That's Only Yesterdays Good Works And For Some Good Works To Be Finished And Done ......................... 48

That's How He Does Help Raise Me On Calls Now ............................................... 49

That Seeks The Lord ............................................................................................... 50

It's On And On ........................................................................................................ 51

Summer Travels, When The Travelling is Done ..................................................... 52

Confessions Of Mental Illness 2002 ...................................................................... 53

Whenever We Were Having Conversations Together ............................................ 54

Of That's Art Works Here ....................................................................................... 55

Good Days And Good Nights .................................................................................. 56

Of Our Sure Testimonies And Of Faith in God Almighty ..................................... 57

Of Holy Writ ........................................................................................................... 58

Wow, Jesus! ............................................................................................................ 59

On That Works And The Only One Given From God Almighty ............................ 60

That's Working On A New Day Everyday .............................................................. 61

LOVE ...................................................................................................................... 62

Some Need To Write ............................................................................................... 63

Of Wifely Duty ....................................................................................................... 64

On Our Holy Marriage For Over 33 Years This Year ........................................... 65

Walking On Rising Sun Avenue ............................................................................. 66

For Now, Call Now ................................................................................................. 67

Of Seeking Prayers ........................................................................................ 68

On To Create More Art Works ...................................................................... 69

Of Life And To Do Certain Things Here........................................................ 70

Poem About That Spirit Of God  And To Do Of That Soul. That God Does Give Me . 71

A Wonderful, Old Friend................................................................................ 72

Out Of The Alley And That's Into Studies  And That's Of My Own Books  And Writings Here ............................................................................................ 73

A Holy Marriage............................................................................................. 74

On Holy Life Here .......................................................................................... 75

Holy Angels And Me ...................................................................................... 76

Author Only SherAnne's Biography ............................................................... 77

Of Influences for Author Only, SherAnne Shea Jubelirer .............................. 78

Fun Facts About Author Only,  SherAnne Shea Jubelirer ............................... 79

O Sweet, Holy Jesus, the Christ..................................................................... 80

Day And Day Light ........................................................................................ 81

By Now........................................................................................................... 82

Of Signs And Wonders Of God Almighty...................................................... 84

# Forward

*We met and commenced our writing careers together in 1986. Married in 1987 writing and loving and striving for holiness and righteousness all the Way to the presence of many books, that we have written.*

*And received publications for. Cherished are our revelations of days of much emotion, we keep on producing and creating our hearts and minds besides for this again and again and with our awareness of God's choices for us very together here.*

*by Jeffrey David Jubelirer*

# Choosing Life And Wisdom Now

I do think my morals have greatly improved since Jeff has come back home now.

Except I do not like my neighbors. That's a hard one. I was always trying to be loving anyhow.

I do feel like I am writing important things and I do have more important things to do than to be so troubled over her sin.

As far as that's mine does have too many children and they have been welcoming and very kind to us, Shea Jubelirer's.

I do love and I am supposed to take that's only my father doing somewhere and that's only my mother doing somewhere.

Our home base has been over in Avalon.

We were all getting together every summer. We will be coming to the New Jersey Shore like 6 visits every year.

We must love and chose to be loving. Do me true love, do me big love and do me great love so I have decided to do so. I must be true to myself here.

" To thine own self be true." As of this writing I am feeling better and better as I write.

Maybe I use I statements too much and are supposed to write more things without I. Choosing

Life maybe necessary now and doing prayers for wisdom often.

The priest said its alright that Jeff and Sherry didn't have children. Except my mother gave Kelly's boys over to us.

Like the Litany of the Precious Blood of Christ says bringing forth virgins.

Perhaps my life maybe necessary for some. I have had a hard time in Philly.

But my father said I am supposed to be tough. Maybe I Will be tougher with maturity.

Guess what? That's good news now. Tim is coming up from Baton Rouge for a visit.

I was telling Brittany that he was cruising and riding along but that's what he was doing!

I do hope he is very smart as they say. He said neighbors near us, they sit!

Life is tough enough. Things do have to be very good for us. I am having to be as a writer and poet.

They said the neighbors. They say they wouldn't and they say I am a certain.

Sure I am a certain kind of person and I am a very good person and I will never give up my efforts to be very good.

Sure, I do certain things now.  And I do come of very good people and that us Shea's and us Keifer's and I work and we work on ourselves everyday.

## *All that I do have to do that now*

Realizing by getting therapy thru Lettie that I am reminded in therapy and that I do like to do this and that I do like to do that and I can take this and I can take that. Recently I remembered that and I was at 9 colleges and universities and Charles Morris Price Business School Of Advertising And Journalism. I earned some 170 college credits almost all B's.

By SherAnne Jubelirer

Monday, July 17, 2017

# On Writings And That's Family

And That's Friends Somewhere

And now working to build more good works and wondering will we get together even if on the phone for more often than now to my liking for my very good siblings.

And of their children since I needed relationships and more friends.

All we need is love.

And that's that.

Us Authors Only were done as that's that and maybe this. That's pretty neat that both of us left anything else to read for all.

# We Need To Get A Way From Philly And Over Around God Almighty

For the poet and I, authors only of love,

We were able to get away to New Jersey, on the shore again

And for a while, we were with my folks who have been wonderfully beautiful

For a stay at my father's home over in Avalon.

And they do very loving things for they do for us.

They had many children likewise.

My mother is beautiful and lovely

And she took us to do shopping for clothes and fashion so that I will look like I had some style and fashion and beauty.

She beautifies me.

I do think that' s sad whenever I see women on television getting older.

I am only one of these women who must do all within my power to quit smoking.

Deal with wrinkles and look and feel so good again.

Lord Jesus, have mercy on us!

I do need to be a beautiful old woman like my mother is

And I do need to keep right on being disciplined and working

And creating successes for us and with Jeff here.

We are creative geniuses and literary geniuses and catholicism has genius.

Holy marriage is 150 and 150 for us.

Likewise I did score that's 145 whenever I was in school. My father has been genius.

Well, we were working, to do that works or a true aspect of the four of us being so done and made of love as well.

On holidays and making holidays together.

Tomorrow night is New Year's Eve.

I do truly wish to have drink or two since I have been so depressed recently,

All I ever do is cry for these days.

Jeff is a poor man and he does need a greater capacity for love.

He says he is terrible at intimacy.

He needs to think again for us here!

With God Almighty, it's all wisdom that's coming up for us right here.

# On Thought and Life Here

O for certain to think of the very name of Jesus.

Of the Christ of love and that's pretty powerful is He indeed!

Each and every new day, learning does happen

And is required that, that is by faith in our Holy One, our great Father God, the One who loves us so.

Yearnings and ponderings of His Will, statutes, precepts and orders.

We must obey

And that will show of our love to Him. We pattern Our life to be like Jesus by worship

And continuing prayers and its through prayers and thee Blessed Mother by working

As we come near to God and He comes near to us always. And by land. we are far and we want to come closer together as that's friends and that's anymore family together here in America.


By Shea Jubelirer

# On Doing The Holy Rosary With Love
# Thru Blessed Mother, Mary Most Holy

Together we prayed

And did prayers whenever we were to

The Holy Catholic Church that holy day

And the only requirement of truth was that

We were of faith in God.

And the idea of love was on ever on our minds

As we were receiving Christ Jesus, the Lord

To give us salvation and of that's eternal life that

Will come for us with God Almighty.

All were welcome at church

And 4 of us stayed to pray the Holy Rosary to

The Blessed Mother of God, Mary,  Most Holy.

After holy mass was offered by Fr. Issac Dominic.

When we were done praying the Holy Rosary.

I exclaimed "that's done, that's finished."


By Shea Jubelirer

November 21, 2014

# That's Mentalities That Had Hope

Struggling to find some peace

And realizing Jesus, the Christ is our peace.

That being Writers and Poets and Artists living

In the city of brotherly love

While we are desiring to create everyday.

Looking for true freedom of thought and thinking

Through certain readings

And certain books.

Wanting to be a greater thinker, I do try to quiet myself.

Together we lay on our bed dreaming on thinking,

Not yet sure how powerful my thoughts can be

While I am a little fearful other's thoughts can influence me so much here.

Though I heard on NPR that there are no thought crimes.

Finding that very assuring for I do remember that of being paranoid

And thinking my address to strangers was out in the open.

I thought they heard my address in my mind whenever I was laying on my bed

And wishing to think more straightly.

Paranoia had set in.

Yet my behavior is acceptable, mostly

And now I am looking at the ethics of my situation here.


By Shea Jubelirer

# O For Thine Ever On Jesus!

Since every moment is thine O Sweet Holy Jesus, I give praise to you…

Sweet Holy Savior of that's mine somewhere.

Truly I Iove you for I was getting that was said for all of us Shea's and us Keifers before You O Thee Sweet Holy Jesus, for you O God did promises of love and wholesomeness and pieces of writing for all and they are gone and far a way and they will come again. That we can truly live someplaces and love one another as they were of love for full well of us up in the Holy Spirit. I already do know the Truth, Jesus, Himself .

And that's well written and all these or those of us Shea's and us Keifer's were already saved by His Blessed, Holy, True Blood for "Christ has died, Christ is risen and Christ will come again."

By Shea Jubelirer

# An Accolade

That's approbation and that's accomplishments.

Being told both of us have what it takes to be

Writers and poets,

Therefore my friends making my life happier now

And more fulfilled.

Needing to read more and more everyday.

Building on our abilities and talents and skills and gifts for writing books

And other writings like articles.

And we have abilities to concentrate and focus.

Do the work consistently

And then things will happen finding things are supposed to be for on my way, for that was said in therapy.

Here is mercy for that's our days

And nights with God Almighty.


By Shea Jubelirer

2002

# To Do That's Due

That does look to God Almighty, for we take

Jesus, the Christ in holy communion seriously and frequently.

We sure do take to do and so very much was already done by us Authors Only, as that's all kinds of writings and any books

At work right here.

And of our books, we do claim that's pretty neat

And that's so cool

That we made such brilliant art works.

And of these our books.

They were made up of thoughts us Authors Only thought so.

Us Authors Only and big thinkers were doing day by day

And of dreams night after night.

So that's due each and every book

That we sure wrote for everyone.

For faith in God Almighty, I do plan to keep that's on.


By Shea Jubelirer

October 6, 2020

# And Of Life and Of That's Love

Tired of trying so hard

And finding depression in my supposed beautiful soul and spirit…

I am so beautiful and pretty

Except I do have concerns of getting older

And that seeking to do the Will of God everyday

And that's as my true will exactly to do like Jesus, the Christ.

Maybe some good sound sleep

And dreams will refresh

And beautify me

And l will make some more prayers for that's family

And that's friends.

And my prayers of loves ease my mind together on that of God Almighty.

And that's love for my Beloved is real

And I do try hard to be true to him.

For faith in Almighty God, I do keep that on.

For the way, that's always true on how I am to thee great American poet, Jeff.

And that's only of my mother doing somewhere and that's only my father doing somewhere.

And that's always true, our loves of one another so very together.

Heaven is that's a goal with Jesus, the Christ forgiving and loving us.


By SherAnne Shea Jubelirer

January 23, 2013

# We Were Even From The Holy Angels!

And to look with God Almighty and the holy angels

And of beauty

And goodness

And truths that our most holy faith is made up of

And we wonder to do for anything or was

Of anything was of that's mine.

I was reminded that's mine.

And we took all over everywhere that we were

And had been of life in many places, an over

This country

And we ever saw America

For I was seeing power and money and freedom, then.

We were coming to the catholic churches

And doing prayers to God Almighty was of priorities.

We put God first everyday.

Now all we need to do is wait on God Almighty to act.

We do know God Almighty does work and so does love

And so that does is me

And us Authors only will persevere

And make prayers for God Almighty to preserve us

And keep us here.


By Shea Jubelirer

July 14, 2020

## *Seeking Jesus and*
## *For a Circle of Loves And Graces*

That's love does reign,

And that's love does rule,

And together we can do all things thru Christ Jesus

Who does strengthen us.

And by the power of the Holy Spirit

We are given power of love in the Kingdom of God.

And of Christ, these gifts of the Holy Spirit, we do receive.

And that will be shown of our love to Him

And we do seek thankful hearts

And are of optimism

And mysticism thru contemplations

And prayers.

And I do ask for God's mercy for all of us

And I do loose great graces on us

And I have been for over doing that

And we will be victorious.

And by love, we will witness of our holy faith in Jesus

And share love

And find understanding of that our loves and life,

We do already know that this is all of God's doing!

For God Almighty is to be ever and by now.


By Shea Jubelirer

By SherAnne Shea Jubelirer

December 18, 2012

# *That's Before To Do A While, That's Us*

Triumph in your eyes of tears

That you spill

Whenever you are sad

You look on to me in silent admiration

Of many poems that were written by

Your deep, brilliant mind saying certainties

And truths.

You were my right-hand man, then.


By SherAnne Shea Jubelirer

## Waking Up One Day

It was as how one day I awakened wondering why

I stayed at this house, my father owned here.

'Cause the houses were so close together

Row upon row.

I often had thoughts about what was around us here

Except I did not know who was near us.

Just that,

That sounded like a ghetto

And many people lived in Lawndale.

What made me think more about the neighbors

Was the fact that I could hear voices

That I thought were theirs.

Except of truth, that's hallucinations

from medicine that I took,

The bible says not the voices of strangers,

They were strangers, mostly,

Just a few of the neighbors talked to us.

A kind of intimate existence behind walls in separate houses,

And us not knowing who lived there.

I truly wished to get along

And I longed for more privacy

And freedom of thought.

I wanted a certain amount of secrecy

And great private things to bring out of my life only

Whenever I wanted to.

I needed to be appreciated for these mysteries of Catholicism

And mysticism as well.

I do realize healing and the power of love does heal.

God is love.

Except more and more I am working and focusing on more of that's mine.

For we sure did do all kinds of good works with our writings and books here.

August 3, 2013

# Of That's Appreciation And
# Of That's Gratitude

I am of appreciation and gratitude for my father and mother for they do that

And they give us that's everything and my father loves that's paid for that's everything else placed

For that's over here. For they sure do, hopefully things and we will get better and better and improve

For a while here. They do these are best for us. We do talk everyday and my folks

Are another holy couple for us. They have been great grandparents since 2018.

We hope all is well and that's well done. We do love my mother and father greatly

And of very good ways we sure do as to do that as we depend On God's ways. They do have friends and family

Like any one else. And they lead full lives and I do realize my mother has a true devotion

To the Blessed Mother, Mary, Most Holy. We love our Catholicism and readings and prayerbooks so very much.

God has been so very good to us and for the love of God and for God's infinite love daily.


By Shea Jubelirer

June 19, 2020

# Working With The Artist's Way Program Here

Trying to get writing again everyday for the Artist's way is

A task that is supposed to restore my creative energies

And creativity and creative genius and literary genius and poetic genius that

I do possess and desire to grow by of doing these tasks here.

Mostly all I do ever do is things on the computer like calls and doing

Research and watching videos. I do need to clean our house and

Jeff does the dishes and I do try to pick up our house but the house-keeping

Rarely gets finished or done. I was talking to someone who suggested

I do keep on working with Facebook fan pages for web traffic and to get

More exposure for our many, many good works of writings and books.

Jeff and I do love one another however, our love must grow deeper

And more true and real. And by now here, we do

Have a holy marriage and of love, we do truly love

One another very together. That's for over 33 years this year.


By Shea Jubelirer


November 12, 2012

Typed July 30, 2020

# Its Show Time and Starring

Perhaps preparation

And being already ready for

Another show has made me reflective

And looking on what words to share

With other writers and poets.

I do have that sense of perfection,

That image of reading my good reads

And works

And appearing with a made up face

And of that seeking the Truth

And what can happen

As truths become learned at Poetry And Literary Forum.

To hope of being fancy

And using words unusually

And looking at language with a love of sound

And all forms of writing

Building on the pages

And necessary becomes thinking that happens

Whenever we sit in our chairs and absorb each presentation,

With some talents and abilities,

We put forth that effort

And take time to present our good works.

Then spiritual roses of poetry will rise up above

The noises out there on the city street

and expansion and growing of such thoughts will come.


By SherAnne Shea Jubelirer

# On That's Love Forever!

And realizing to do that or this right here and that's to apply that's love

Everywhere and that's love to come anywhere. And as likely, the true

And real answer is love, that's love forever. Its hard to get love, except

I do got some who do give love each within our own ways and giving love

And ways of love and before that's mine give that's deals and that's agreements

And that's assignments, that's love is all so we try to seek after to do this of love

Here and we will do that's only of love here. Is anything of newness here for you?

For a few brief moments. I do faith reflections for that's hold up for a while and of my attractive, pretty face realizes that I do need to create love again.

That's only love forever!


By Shea Jubelirer

October 28, 2019

## That's Tasks To Do

Maybe beginning to write of how I must think

And build some kind of breakthrough for my writings

And very good writing career so that returning to work

Will happen before this question of how I will put all this writing and all that writing together.

And I do realize I would rather socialize then work.

And thousands and thousands of pieces of writing are

In my possession and I have learned spiritually

That I can have Jesus!

Thanks be to God Almighty for that.


By Shea Jubelirer

# As A Teacher, Maybe I Could Have Been

Just only one day

When I was taking a walk with Truth, that pup

And I was asking for God's Mercy,

I was walking past the church

And I said Hi to Fr. Joe Watson

And he said hi to me, then when I was at the store by the Holy Catholic Church,

I had already asked for God's Mercy for

I was buying myself these light cigarettes

And I began walking home again,

That's when I was talking to a school boy

And told him I am an author, writer and poet.

He asked whether he could help.

So I told him I needed a typist, secretary and maid.

He said he could type except I told him, I couldn't afford to pay him.

He said he would type for free.

I told him, no, I would need money for him.

We were walking the same way at the same time

And our conversation was lively.

I said he needed good luck, thank you.

I said that for out on the street

And I bet everyone heard that.

Then he said he'll see myself tomorrow

And I coolly said take care.

And the walk was exhilarating

That walking, doing all that

That does me very good whenever

We walk with God.

And I do think I made that boy think.

It was a great experience

And I do think I was supposed to be a teacher more than once or twice

Whenever I was a teacher long ago.

By Shea Jubelirer

February 28, 2013

# *Of That's Works And Online*
# *A perspective with God Almighty*

Frustrations in my mind of holy faith

That needs soundness

And silence

And peace now,

Daily overwhelmed by too much information

And recovering focus by working on the computer often

And rich with ideas

And abundance of thought and thinking here

Yet needing organization, clarity

And structure.

Basically that was how things were

Whenever I try to get some perspective.


June 24. 2002

By SherAnne Shea Jubelirer

## Of To Do That's Faith And Graces

Seeking the truth Himself ever again,

That Jesus God by listening to the Holy Scriptures

Of Jesus

And trying to stay calm

And learning Jesus abideth forever.

I am thinking while I am looking on.

# *Good Days*

Regular work day

And being on the mend again.

Pursuing goals of beauty, truth and reason.

Actually Avon, poetry and prayers.

A good day held much strength

A love grew deeper

A friendship increased my ability to call myself

A writer and poet.

This was of hope on my way working at home

And becoming.

To win is key,

To smoothe out, to smoothe out is my desire!


2002

By SherAnne Shea Jubelirer

# An Experience Of That's Love

That Seeking of feelings of love

And thinking thoughts of love is first a process

To get there.

Thunder storms

And sun showers, above in the sky

Air and gentle breezes lightly touching on before my skin.

"Hope in a jar."

Applications of cream after being heated

And wanting to let the tepid, cool water splash down

My body

And its covering for my head.

Giving me wetness and moisture

And coolness here to repeat process

And come to sit in chair by an open window.

Splashing in summer light scent of Avon cologne,

Sweet Honesty.

Trust in God, necessary.


By Shea Jubelirer

# A Poor City Neighborhood

I am feeling so put under over my neighbors,

They are none for friendship and love

And Jeff is so domineering

And the catholic church suffers.

I am just 43 years old as I write this,

I should not have to worry about that today

Or anytime soon.

I am a rebel at heart over and beyond my neighborhood.

They are out with us Authors Only.

I gave a little bit with doing Avon for 14 years in Lawndale

And we sure were offering our books

And I sure was doing prayers anyhow.

Particularly since I was in the Carmelite program for 3 years

And we were studying Catholicism

And mysticism and prayers and contemplations,

I will not accept under their souls

Or for anything over to do finer here.


By Shea Jubelirer

July 23, 2002

# To Realize That Everyday Of Life Right Here

To realize how to daily do things in keeping on to improve our life

That's to be made very together in God Almighty as that's a real quest.

And that's love is to do for one another by thinking and dreams and prayers here.

We do try to do prayers continually

And we pray that everyday.

We read and we write and we do on our computers often.

We were made by God Almighty

As us Authors only, Writers and Poets, Artists

And Intellectuals and Scholars and Philosophers, messengers, a little bit here.

Jeff likes its politicking

And I was liking to evangelize,

We love to call the prayer lines,

I was told I was for overdoing that by the priests.

And whenever we work, we do take on too much work to do right here.

And we do like, my father and I that we are too much of that.

And my mother's thing is to do. They say she has too many children, now grown and gone far away.

We will see wholesomely, gone and far and every where

And yes, we will do.

As an Author that has to do that,

I will do that. All that I do have to do with Jeff, thee great poet!

As always we will keep on looking for ways to improve

And to be good and to make better of things for ourselves and of that's best for us.

We hope to better to do while making that's best for us and God Almighty is all kinds of these things and He is so good and better and best. And he is beyond people that won't give.

# *A Drug Addict's Prayer in 1999*

Whenever the 3 of us were getting high during the 1990's

Of penance I do offer my suffering to the Holy One.

To partake of suffering is sweet sorrow over sin.

How on fire I must be of this psychic pain

I am enduring.

Yet knowing hopefully with God Almighty,

We find joy in suffering so that

We may be eternally glad.

# Of Sufferings And Psychosis

A Medical Condition

Suffering over those voices in my head here.

Feelings of frustration well up within me.

Needing medicine the only answer.

Needing self esteem to over come.

Feelings of shame over being ill.

Yet having a great deal of above normalcy and normalcy

With my family and love.

At times not letting myself hate others who hate me

Because of my suffering.

I will forgive these.

I will be strong.

I am stronger than any other voice

And I am way more of intelligence than any voices.

Wishing I truly could love myself

And overcome that.

Post Script:

2 doctors confirmed that, prescription drugs do cause hallucinations.

That's so much improved by now.


By Shea Jubelirer

2002

## Jeff and Sherry in our beginnings of writings that was.

I asked "do you say by faith?"

He said, "by faith and experience

We take the highway of truth."

I do wonder with him together

On of our intelligences of being enough to be

Book Writers and Poets.

That's of joy to have the mind of Christ,

God willing for us here…

We will have work to do.


By Shea Jubelirer

## To My Beloved

For me to be in love with you

is a very good experience.

For I will always treasure for

You can light up my smile inside my heart.

Whenever you desire for

Our life together shall be sweet with

Thoughts of God, for in holiness

Our love is an everlasting testimony of

What God can do…


By Shea Jubclircr

8-1-2020

# *Writer Do What Writers Do!*

I am the artist at work coming

Up with and recognizing good ideas,

That flows and that sounds good

and that's being with

all of my best friends.

Perhaps that's only in my heart right now

And yet hopefully doing the same things for

The ones are these my siblings.

My soulmate also recognizes this, that's all, too.

They are best friends from way back.

Love must be on truths now

And always.

Life must happen, that's very good.

That's another six siblings with God Almighty.

And likewise I am only the first born of us.


By Shea Jubelirer

November 10, 2000

## Vanity Fair

That's Vanity Fair flickering forth with fire in the candles

And an attempt to overcome this.

Whenever in days that's past I gazed into mirrors of

My own making to do here.

However I am longer before, God willing bought

By the Most Holy Precious Blood now of Jesus

That flows and that covers our souls, minds and spirits for

For we are on God's own…

Hopefully saved by graces of Jesus who does that.


By Shca Jubclircr

7-31-2020

# Of Often Taking Walks In Out In Lawndale

Whenever I was walking so I took walks for that does myself

And I am such an exception.

That I do believe God does me for some more writings

And for more success.

However, one day I was testing the neighbors

So I put the raindeer fallen over out on the lawn.

And they don't care, they didn't pick her up

And they didn't care.

I was testing them neighbors.

They didn't know or prove worthy of friendship

And trust and before that, and of me that's truly that I have been while

I was here

Ever since 1993.

And books wise, we are reaching very far a way geographically

And we are doing so far, and so good in life and wondering

How far is heaven?


By Shea Jubelirer

Typed July 18, 2020

# On Beauty To Do Here

And so beauty and beautiful thoughts, I do desire.

On Wednesday, I will do some shopping to get

Beauty deals and to look good.

Like shimmering cream eye shadows

And eye liners

And perfect foundation

And beauty products that will help.

God is so good

And God is to do my life, always!

For Jesus, we do trust in you!

For I truly was becoming a devotional, catholic

And evangelical writer and poet and author only.

And is by faith so now I learned of myself, that's new.

I was receiving actual graces

Whenever I received Jesus actually present in the Holy Liturgy.

Since I have lived near Saint William's True, Holy Roman Catholic Church.

Coming to church regularly has been my quest

 And of my destiny in God.

Likewise, writings and readings make up a great deal of all my life.

Since I have been doing that since 1985.

And I do love being an Author as a Who's Who that has

Sanctions and great status.

But a writing profession is often a lonely occupation and focus.

And I do love best to read my writings and books

When they have been published bend finished or of that's well done.

And made by me.

I have been called an outstanding writer and also a very accomplished

# Author Just needed or wanted more contact with others socially

Or professionally.

I do like to drink beer

And I do like cosmetics and some men.

I do truly need a decent, professional girlfriend but

I am unable to find her now.

I do got a few friends, that I have been calling

But they are no shows.


By Shea Jubelirer

August 8, 2020

# Days of Believing The Lord Jesus Christ
# and To love Him So

Reading Bible Scriptures at Saint William's True, Holy Roman Catholic Church and making great Prayers and occasionally I am making new friends. I just have so many acquaintances as well.

I was already at church on Monday and on Tuesday when Father Joe Watson said Mass. I probably will show up at church all week. I am hopefully getting a spiritual advisor. I was beginning to think Father Joe Watson and I will maybe be contemporary's. That's now come and gone, such ideas…

I am sure saying prayers for such possibilities of whatsoever I may want and probably I am loved every so often. And I do try to love everyone and I pray for everyone and place before all of mine for they been and live all over everywhere else. God is always and everywhere. And he was strong for how we could do our life together by coming to church regularly. I truly loved him and I do learn through the Catholic Church.

The priests are and were very beloved at our catholic church, Saint William's. I am truly Beginning to like living by myself for now except as of this writing Jeffrey David Jubelirer, the love of my very life has returned and come home together and really for God. God is ever before me with my little blonde buff cocker spaniel named Truth. Who Is requested and of that I ask Saint Francis of Assisi to pray for him, a gone, gone dog That we used to have and loved so much. And God is Ever faithful. O Jesus, we trust in Thee! And look for new ideas and new loves to come. That's looking for new interests and things that I am to do for this all here. We know God is so good and we seek to do anymore good and to be good and great and hopefully as excellent moments may come Like whenever I am at Saint William's, our holy church or visiting my mother and father at the New Jersey Shore so together. So I am so finished and finishing is greater for me And Jeff is done. Families aren't perfect and out of Philly, kids starting are good except I feel like saying tell them kids to get out of my hair. Beauty that I have been with hope and grace to try and take care of ourselves and graces abounding.

For we authors only do bind ourselves to Jesus, the Christ and Jeffrey David Jubelirer is A jew for Jesus and I am a lay catholic mystic waiting on God to act for another mystical gift that He can give and that He always does. Trust in God and great faith and great love, that's necessary and of efforts made by us here.

# History Of Love Of Good Fridays And Penance

O what a happy day! That recording of that song, I must find. When our glorious Jesus Took away all of our sins. And that reason being is His Great and Holy Blood has saved all of us from our despicable and negative ways. I love being a charismatic, catholic Christian. For 3 years, I studied with the Third Order Carmelites. They are known for prayer to make prayers and contemplate and meditate on holy thoughts. "Jesus, Mary Joseph, I love you, save souls!" I was so happy on Good Friday. Church was so uplifting And I was happy that my humanity and sin was paid for, bought and covered by Jesus when He died for us on the cross. Even of my afflictions, I must overcome. I am saved by graces, by Jesus.

# Doing And To Do Spiritual Disciplines in God Almighty

Regarding seeking the TRUTH truths that I experience and perceive of all of my life, wherein or whenever I was coming to the Catholic Church like holy days of Obligation and during weekdays whenever I could get to church. I do believe I was helped by God. And protection is important and hopefully the Holy Saints in heaven and holy angels do help us. Certain priests always have helped cleanse and purify me of my Sin by telling me to pray and say prayers for holy purity and graces and courage and through the sacrament of reconciliation on a regular basis whenever I wanted to talk to the priests. And they helped make me more aware of myself and Jesus. I was likewise trying to grow a great deal with my prayer life as well. My wholesome self, heart, mind, body and spirit is experiencing remission over sin and overcoming the past such as mistakes I may have made. I am very good @understanding and forgiveness and I do freely forgive easily and was making prayers for all kinds of graces and holy angels for all of us Shea's and Keifer's and several others including the priests and some of the nuns of all of our catholic church. One of the nuns. Sister Jamie who was good to me gave me a catholic resource list so that I could write a theology book for my fourth book. Except paperwork is easily lost or thrown out. She also taught instructions and said I was way beyond them at the bible study since I have studied the bible for such a long time.

However with all of that I am suffering often since Jeffrey attends so many meetings to deal with his manic depression and to work on his excellent poetry. He works on himself regularly. We both do. I must realize I am wherever I am supposed to be, and whenever I am to realize I do have to do that and here is where we can live and I am to do the writing that I then do have to do that for now here.

Yet its true I am supposed to overcome and get rid of a part of reality as it does not matter or work for me and rather wholistically turn back to God so I choose hereby to live wholesomely with no destructive drug and no destructive neighbors and to do beyond Many people except the ones that are that were good to us and I was made to make a choice of Jesus, the Christ instead! Jeff has his questions.

My first two publishers, too, didn't pay. Only my mother, only my father only Jeff help provide for me. They are holy and they are doing great. They like to be likewise. I do get some money from U.S. government as my source of income. just only enough to pay for myself. Living the writing life is often without much pay, however when my publishers get a marketing program together for my books and Jeff's books maybe we will make some money. And the holy life is trusting God that He will provide. That's the reason I keep trying to make some money on the web. With this indeed, my life is often frustrating. We deserve pay for our books! I think my everything takes a great while, believe me! And I am supposed to mean for a while for myself. So I make choices of believing God and believing myself while I await and keep.

# *Thinking And Dreaming Of God's Love*

All of these and concerns of mine only

Were pale

And gone and unconsequential

Whenever I focus and fix my eyes on into light of Christ's deep abiding Love being

What it is

And while I was to dwell upon all lightness

And mystical imaginings or of private revelations

That God Almighty does give me and that I do believe God can give and Holy Spirit

anointings given by gifts of the Holy Spirit

and that I have found inside of His Love that overflows freely

Whenever our souls, hearts and minds feel full of soundness and clearer thinking

And I am experiencing complete freedom with His Love inside Of me

absolutely thinking and working with the Lord God and with dreams of Him.


By Shea Jubelirer

# April 2010 Things Were Happening Of Then And Of Doing In Life

Regarding seeking the truth and truths that I experience and perceive of that's to be of all my life, I perservere for I have been to Mass very often and confession regularly. Making confessions to the priests has helped cleanse me by recommendations of prayer and that Sacrament of Reconciliation and made me more aware myself. I am likewise trying to grow a great deal with my prayer life as well. Sacramentals of the Holy Catholic Church are great experiences and of the will of God and they do create graces for us holy, good catholics.

My wholesome self, heart, mind, body and spirit is experiencing remission over sin and overcoming the past. I am good @understanding and forgiveness, and seeking wisdom through knowledge and scriptures and making prayers for all kinds of graces and holy Angels for all of us Shea's, us Keifer's and several others. However, despite that I am suffering loneliness often since Jeffrey attends so many meetings to deal with his manic depression and to work on his excellent poetry. I so only wish he could never leave and God willing, for Jeff is the love of my life forever.

By Shea Jubelirer

# Growing And Learning and Living In the Same Way Since That's Only Yesterdays Good Works And For Some Good Works To Be Finished And Done

February 8, 2006

I did study with the Third Order Carmelities for three years in the Catholic Church I learned that thru prayers and contemplations that mysticism with God, Jesus and the Holy Spirit is of possibility. That is real motivation to make prayers and to contemplate on certain topics or that of certain things to remember that and God or Jesus or the Holy Spirit HimSelf.

February 12, 2006

When we awakened today, the snow had fallen. So my darling husband went to the Store to stock up on groceries and we were loving beings inside of our home here. Right now, all is well with us. On Friday, the 10th I worked for 10 hours that day. I was Typing up Jeff's second book, DEAR GOD AND PERFECT MOMENTS. I think that it is so excellent! I am very, very proud of him that he wrote that. Really, I love to work on the computer. I think being on the web is so interesting, mostly for listening to calls and Reading articles.

Jeff was just saying we are being used by people. I really wonder if it is true or of if people are evil. Helene screamed at me today because I said I was prolife. Unfortunately, she is fighting with me. Truly I am a lover and doer and I never love a fight. Avoid the fighter, overcome the fight.

I truly would like to try to be more loving. I do think love is the answer and my first Book, POETIC MEDITATIONS FROM AN ANOINTING OF THE SPIRIT, and second Book, MEDITATIONS OF A POETESS AND PRAYER WARRIOR, were very sweet Books, and well, that first book that I wrote says that's love is the answer. God loves every one of us and the prayer line and my father told me, I can love everyone. And keep that's on for all of us of that's mine and this is mine, that has been everywhere.

And some like doctors, brothers, priests were very liked by me. I often enjoy talking to other professionals and our family is all professionals. We got 7 MBA's and two writers and poets! O, for work and love!

# That's How He Does Help Raise Me On Calls Now

God to do all that walking that I have been doing and for a great while meant for me. Since I was made Author only, Writer and Poet, I have been doing writings since 1985. I have so very much to show of good works for that. How to do very little is real and my writings and books were real true as I have already written and published many things. And I can do all kinds of things for that's only my father's doing that he has told me that, so that I do all kinds of thoughts and thinking and on things in my notebooks.

I do realize Sherry's things are only one day every day. I do have on that work day and on that holy day daily and every day. I do things on paper and in books. And now online is 64 articles that's written and published for I have done that. And that's of my books were written and published and made available online.

My books were made only in America as an Author that does of the truth and my truths and beauty and things of faith and by prayers I have made by God's graces that were sown of me as I write that which things that were before me or what was, could be written. I have to do this one here on December 3, 2015. An author has to be eloquent and exquisite and elegant.

And I do love to create beautiful things as I write of that, that happens for God's infinite goodnesses and infinite graces and mercies. Ok, things are very good here.


By SherAnn Shea Jubelirer

December 3, 2015

# That Seeks The Lord

Sadness and joy somehow feeling both feelings

With the moment

While I truly am listening to the beautiful music,

That is on my television

And making prayers

And while I am reading my bible right along

With this holy day today.

Hopefully I will feel good for a while

And believe and trust God that all ought to be fine, with all well, for Jesus does love us

And God is looking to see whatever we may be doing

And big thinkers right here

And dreams of happy moments that we can do that together or this.

By working and making an effort

And earning our ways with hope.


By Shea Jubelirer

# *It's On And On*

A spiritual awakening does happen often

When I begin on the beginning of my day

And prayers are made

And hope in God rules.

Always to seek God is all diligent efforts I make

And God does reward myself by me learning

New things day by day and of life and perceptions of life and certain loves and friends are desired

And I do think I can grow to be more independent

And God will provide

And take care of myself and all others. He will watch over us. As I sought meaningful conversations,

That were supposedly made in heaven

And forgiveness is a great deal

And I so do pray to be forgiven and given peace,

A most precious gift.

And prayers for increases of holiness and righteousness

In God for I made prayers and of correct things

And transfixing my holy life and writing life and beauty

Life is consistently done and thankfully for all that I do

Have to do that and again beginning now I will reapply

My motivation and freedom and finish very much work

And accomplish something with God Almighty daily

And those holy angels.

March 24, 2016

# *Summer Travels, When The Travelling is Done*

Together the two poets planning our summer travels

Such as trips to the New Jersey Shore again and again

By walking on the beach

And swimming in the deep, mysterious sea.

We will be going out for dinner often.

Hopefully we will be inspired enough to write

Some more poetry

Or even short stories during our days Whenever

We stay inside my folk's beautiful home

Since we want to stay out of the Sun

And doing readings will be a constant pre-occupation

And relaxation

And good sound sleep and dreams of God's rest here.

And that's all for now.


By Shea Jubelirer

# Confessions Of Mental Illness 2002

Awakened by my cat,

I am suffering but all of us suffer

Now and then.

I may be the only one with those voices but

We all suffer sometimes.

Today can be much better.

Things were only my feelings taking shape.

Whenever I do think of how distressing life can be.

What do I mean by this?

I mean I was in certain ways.

If I do let myself worry,

I can find plenty to concern me,

Simply put may be some of the things I do with Jesus

And my prayer books are that

I am only learning to be more Christian.

I do seek a path of perfection.

I have a long way and far to go.

My prayer books tell me so much!

That's the reason why I must keep on being strong in my faith, so

That I will please God Almighty in faith.


By Shea Jubelirer

# *Whenever We Were Having Conversations Together*

Yapping at my friends

And family, and having conversations and fun.

Talking to another artist on the phone.

Thinking of things to say

And having of the day over.

Of that being sure to see these words and ideas manifested by faith in God Almighty.

That's communications and media here essential in beginning.

Writers and poets talking.

Words flying about—deep thought coming out.


By Shea Jubelirer

# Of That's Art Works Here

By now, I must make mention this is truly like Amy Grant whomever my father so favored her and her music, that I am now playing that record.

Well, this is my father's world and I was given to do for anything to do before the books, we were writing and preparing manuscripts for publishers to publish our good works.

The poet, Jeffrey David Jubelirer has written a great deal and he has been very prolific of all that poetry.

And of all that I can do this evening by writing this right here.

And as lonely and by myself as I may be, I can be mighty good.

For my folks that great couple where 2009 that's for sure, they were two greats living on and they were here at my place today.

I am full of gratitude.

And gladness for my folks and I am very good. Do you, my dear readers believe of my visions of whatsoever I do see? God will give for I would hope so now. This is another book because I keep writing without getting typing done. However, that will come. I do write creative non-fiction mostly of love and fruits of the Holy Spirit and gifts of the Holy Spirit.

And thoughts of Jesus are that then I must do. Hope all is well.

Good night!


By SheAnne Shea Jubelirer

# Good Days And Good Nights

 Ever learning and that's coming up to truths

And true things.

Looking at current realities

And realizing that there is time to develop more and more

That being hopeful for future glory

And doing necessary things through prayers for self-sufficiency

And God's infinite graces are sufficient for our life together.

Trusting certain people

And realizing some do like me.

Trying to feel good, no matter what…

Through prayers for greater talents

And intelligence and wisdom

In all probability wisdom within our souls will grow though holiness

And work

That being strong willed

And willingness within us

Through prayers for all to gain hope in God Almighty.


By Shea Jubelirer

# Of Our Sure Testimonies And Of Faith in God Almighty

We do testify

And desire for the Richard Author Shea

Family to receive this mission's statement

That will be applicable forever

And written on December 31, 2007.

All of the Shea's are to work together out

Of the wells of salvation perhaps holy fear of God and trembling for salvation

And best kinds of life

And living to have shown and give all kinds of goodness

And love to one another because that was

The Way we were raised.

And we all win to be fulfilled of fruits

And gifts of the Holy Spirit.

And again of the anointing of the Holy Spirit is our constant and consistent prayers for ourselves and one another, now covered in the Blood of Jesus, the Christ and the words of our testimonies shall empowered.

Each of us to be overcomers in life.


Notes By Shea Jubelirer

December 31, 2007

# *Of Holy Writ*

Writing for my life and living for God, our King.

I do truly ask Him that I will never

Be separated from Jesus, My Savior.

King of my heart, soul and spirit.

I have been asking God for great graces

For myself and for my wholesome, holy

And righteous and holy, only family.

And I do make prayers for my friends.

I already readily do realize life has so much

More to offer than whatever I can find on here.

And I do love Jeff but he refuses to talk to myself some days.

That frustrates me, truly I say things to him, I didn't always mean out of frustration.

O Lord God give him a new heart for me.

I am so sad and I do cry often.

By now, that's wisdom, whatever wisdom God has

Given me will show things can only get better.

And I am even better and full of goodness, indeed

And I am a beautiful person, but some

People don't see that, I do suppose.

I am only supposed to do that and this is

Together, O Jesus, come to me and win

My nights and days. Holy Scriptures say

This day is holy to the Lord.

My mother said every day is a holy day.

By Shea Jubelirer

February 7, 2013

# *Wow, Jesus!*

How I love Him so very much here.

Or too much to do as far as doings writings

and doing readings is my stand by for us.

And sowing peace is supposed to help me.

That's just some thoughts, I was thinking

To help me live the writing life here.

 Thanks for remembering me

 And realizing I will do.

 Us Shea's and us Keifer's, we'll do.

 We'll see that's hopefully.


By Shea Jubelirer

# On That Works And The Only One Given From God Almighty

For the truth and when God becomes my ultimate reality, we will be so strong in faith for him, that trusting him will come supernaturally and my life is for God since I have given him, my life.

That all I do need to do will happen for best and reasons like mystical reasons will come thru whenever I am doing for my contemplations and prayers.

Yet God works in mysterious ways and he uses magical things, too.

So I do hope for deep inner peace and beauty and for our minds

More lucidity for our minds while we are thinking

And wherever we may be. That's only to be here, yes,

Jesus, the Christ, You are the answer and peace of our souls and spirits and life.


By Shea Jubelirer

Devereaux

April 20, 2013

# That's Working On A New Day Everyday

On that's only routine, everyday.

Of doing routine things that must be done

And things that we do, to do each

And to do everyday for now.

First, God Almighty with prayers made daily that were done here.

Then I made myself already,

Ready now. After that, I will be walking to get

Just 3 cigarettes

And waxing with a Chinese woman on Rising Sun Avenue

So a visit to Dollar General is in order to get cash only here.

And basically this is a great new day.

God's mercies are so new every morn.

And to think hopefully we can do that's goals here.

For we have been authors and big thinkers right here.

And that's final, discerning always this time is for now.

We sure do.


By Shea Jubelirer

March 11, 2020

# LOVE

Wildly chasing a jewish love, and he wants that for us being above the sound of laughter heard in the still of the night. I am thinking of the way I must gather more strength and grow in wisdom to endure the pickiness of my mother and my insane mate of perhaps true religious thought without understanding for a time, by many, even if I truly do of my possession have only the best of intentions and I was seeking to do spiritual works of mercy except for now I realize everyone is taken care of so only prayers are necessary and maybe or hopefully some development of some more friends is what I do want. Yet we are understanding that everyone has a vice or bad habit, none are free of the flesh. While I am praying to get stronger, more capable to walk spiritually among the shadows on their faces, and freedom is out on the street though I don't know if others have any graces better than love of life at home that I do have and graces are given and acquired by coming to the catholic churches and receiving the sacramentals. For indeed, the sacraments are sources of graces for us.

For these few brief hours of happiness when I look into your eyes, realizing you may not see the true reality of greater things coming in God Almighty now hidden until eternal prayers can make way for higher things to be experienced and with understanding so I will try to make my imagination upon the depth and profoundness of the moment, and while showing another love, who is my sweet father made smooth upon the chunks of ice crunched methodically as you put the glass on the table, rhythmically waiting for my revelations of self and love to be experienced on and on and he is farther on and of great love, for that's Sherry's parents with our conversations and far readings and understandings and graces of God who helps us. And we make prayers for all of us from a far. And we agreed its forever and good love is required. And we have yearnings for friendship and realizing good friends are hard to find. Guess, I must keep on reaching out and sowing for friends and family like always and I am doing anything so beautiful, truly. And we always work on ourselves and try to improve.

By Shea Jubelirer

## Some Need To Write

Of desire I often wish to create,

By an urge for expression to make prose and poetry,

Revealing and beautiful

With high hopes of accomplishments

Giving us thinking of satisfaction and peace in God

And giving us knowledge of the power of God and the wisdom of God

Whenever we are receiving Christ Jesus in the Catholic Church.

Whenever I need to grow into a higher state of being and supposed

To do gracefully and easily and know God is and ready to forgive

We trust He does!

By how I do make words flow and I do like to think and ideas will do

Upon page before pages

Through this mystical process called poetry and prose.

Its very important for us suppose I am truly a lay catholic mystic and visionary

That loves God in my own days for things to do before

I am trusting God's Ways.

And dreamers with prescriptions, we do dream and on and on.

And we do believe. That's enough and more to do will come to be.


By Shea Jubelirer

# *Of Wifely Duty*

Experiences of Catholicism and Judaism such faiths for the two of us,

Encouragement we give

And prayers we do

And receiving counsel

I tell of God's graces, sufficient for us in our lives.

We must be faithful

And make our stand on the Word of God.

For in prayers,

Our reality is reasoned and of great writings and full lives

And takes place with understanding.

O God let thy mercies come

And help us

Whenever we are weary.


By Shea Jubelirer

# On Our Holy Marriage For Over 33 Years This Year

That experience I was having of our relationship and

Holy marriage is only growing more uniquely of that being together and that's done by therapy and days and nights of our life

Together with one another wanting so much to love the other one and receiving a call from Tim Shea, our

Brother was of importance and graces for us thinking

Our thoughts and experiencing that faith we build of work and love complicated maybe and too many unwanted people around us yet this is together for we

Will persevere and seek of God, Jesus and of the Holy

Spirit every day and I do realize again and again how

My life is non-negotiable and I must cry whenever

I am hurt instead of getting angry cause people seem anti-social and they seem average or just normal on Has brook and Devereux and yet I was doing reading that I must try and mind my own business as always for doing.

For I would above normally be of social life and of best values of our books, that we have written and made preparations of.

And of my thoughts after having been called a genius

By several others who cared for me. I do think everything is interesting that I do read or write or look at on the computer so that does while trusting God is my source that is now and of brilliance is my pre-occupation with Him and dreams for all that God can give. For each and every day work is accomplished

And prayers and contemplations and priorities are made with God Almighty here.


By Shea Jubelirer

# *Walking On Rising Sun Avenue*

Walking down city streets

Getting my walk on in God Almighty.

Cool air on my face makes my eyes water

And tear and I am feeling alive here.

We were walking for 25 minutes stopping at Seapot Inn for

A seltzer water and coca cola.

Refreshing taste of my drink.

My husband concerned for my desire to be around people gathered in a bar

On Rising Sun Avenue.

I am just wanting to hang out together,

By my need of somewhere to belong

And to be

And to do things together for now.


By Shea Jubelirer

November 24, 2002

## For Now, Call Now

Seeking to maintain my spirituality and beauty and my intellect and physical health and asking that God has plans and ideas for us Authors only on how to do that or maybe for this here. Realizing we are only writers and poets and intellectuals and scholars that must keep on the good works we love to do right here.

And of importance is doing spiritual works of mercy and I seek ways to do spiritual works of mercy for others and all, I do believe spiritual works of mercy is of the way to reach heaven and Jesus, the Christ.

And to make everything done with great love.

By Shea Jubelirer

April 27, 2017

# Of Seeking Prayers

December 3, 2015

And prayers made with fasting to watch and pray

And for these books, certain things of God and made

Were moments with God alone as that seeking of Jesus and I remember that of my spiritual works of mercy and by prayers made for others and ones us Shea's and us Keifer's and prayers of fruits of the Holy Spirit and by prayers of gifts of the Holy Spirit like the spirits of knowledge and understanding and wisdom.

Prayers daily for strength and wisdom, for the joy of the Lord is my strength!

And that's pretty powerful

And that's wise of God. For Jesus is our God! For God is working for us as we fast and pray.


By Shea Jubelirer

# On To Create More Art Works

Now upon this day for

Day by day I am only to begin again to do

A great deal more writing, I only see that

I truly do look for more to do for I would do that for I do believe God Almighty has called and chosen

And He has anointed me as an Author only, writer and poet.

I sure was anointed of the Holy Spirit whenever I was reading my bible

And reaching the prayer lines.

As a holy, devout practicing Catholic, Christian.

As a Catholic Author, I was sensing and feeling the presence of God.

Practically seeing this anointing of the Holy Spirit. God is so good

And life is so good. Right now all of my life is very lonely because Jeffrey David Jubelirer, the poet has left me again. Maybe I have done some imperfection for I am seeing someone tonight. That turned out, he didn't show. I was on the phone talking to guys. Except I wanted Jeff back first, I had fear of the Lord and by now we have made very good on our holy marriage again.

And our love is strong and holy.


By Shea Jubelirer

# *Of Life And To Do Certain Things Here*

Some won't say

Some may be glad

And would understand that over

And above family were who have enough money to travel.

Yet I am must stay here,

Couldn't go because of money

But I will be good willed since I do realize

Maybe I will have many more good days with loved ones and friends.

Though I may be the only one for certain.

Hey, you know certain things, then.


By Shea Jubelirer

# Poem About That Spirit Of God And To Do Of That Soul. That God Does Give Me

That soul of mine likes to think.

Am I being too focused on myself?

Because that's written that Spirit is God's Spirit in the Holy Scriptures.

Dare I say that soul of mine?

Perhaps I do for this very holy day today.

With such a longing for English literature, poems are only one genre'.

I have success with poetry.

And my books do tell me of writing articles as well.

Writing a novel has long been a dream.

Perhaps I can write everything good.

As a writer and poet, Author Only.


By Shea Jubelirer

November 18, 2002

# *A Wonderful, Old Friend*

I am lucky I have a friend who is artist.

She helps me feel freer.

I am tired of compromising.

People are difficult at best.

Helene called at 1:20 PM.

I was irritated with her.

I am trying to understand that of myself here.

Why am I so up hung up on time?

And of my IQ points so often made mention of here?

And I did score that's 145 whenever I was in school. My father was a genius.

Honestly I did score a 144 and my folks said add 1 point,

Since I do great deal of doing writings and doing readings and working on the computer here.

Probably because I do value intelligence as much as I do fine here.

Its very important to us.

And that's necessary here.


By SherAnne Shea Jubelirer

# Out Of The Alley And That's Into Studies
# And That's Of My Own Books
# And Writings Here

Listening briefly to sounds of children outside

Playing in the backyards

And alley.

Birds chirping up higher in the stratosphere

Just background noise

And sounds

By my open window on the second floor of my old house

And I am feeling like I can be at peace here

In this world

My corner of my study and library with

My beloved about to work on

The computer after I have made calls to my Dad.

Liking my feelings right now,

Liking peace floating above like beyond a river,

Comfortable in my study and library

And reading books here.


By Shea Jubelirer

# *A Holy Marriage*

Days fly by I wonder

Will I ever be with someone again?

I truly wanted thee Poet.

I loved him so even if he smacked me.

I was always forgiving him even when he wouldn't answer

My questions or statements of life.

I forgive him today since I am only playing on the phone.

That's how I can be reached to talk of our books

For right now, or prayers.


By: SherAnne Shea Jubelirer

# On Holy Life Here

And I am only keeping right on doing spiritual disciplines day by day,

Night by night. I seek to create a very constant or consistent prayer life

For us in Jesus's Sweet, Holy Name. I so want to be good and to do good,

Because God, the Holy One is so very good.

Jesus, infinite goodness pray for all us Shea's and us Keifer's and for

Whomever reads these my good works.

Holy God, Mighty God, Holy Immortal God, please pray for us!

We are holy, good Catholics

And we wanted ever to be righteous and holy, like Jesus!

I do likewise desire to make recordings of the Holy Scriptures of Jesus on

And with the Holy Angels,

They will protect, comfort and maybe even provide for us.

O how I do believe things of God!

May God uplift our thoughts and thinking to things that are to do of Him

And of optimism and as it is in heaven.

Whenever I read of mysticism, its difficult reading

And yet you O God do show of mysticism thru

The mystical Body of Christ and mystical Blood of Christ Jesus.

Whenever we come to the liturgy of the Holy Mass.

The priests do greatly indeed.

They have been real professionals, truly.

I do come to confession regularly and I am forgiven and my conscience is very right.

O praise, honor, glory and love even forever more for God Almighty, our King!


By SherAnne Shea Jubelirer

December 16, 2012

# *Holy Angels And Me*

Thoughts moving across my brain, where does that say for anything to do here?

And I awaken to make me think higher things of God Almighty.

I must think of truth and mystical things.

Understanding of Cherubs,

All wings

And the Seraphs,

All eyes.

Am I longing to escape the drudgery of everyday

And hard reality

And long to see and give love more,

And know that's more?

Do I only wish love and knowledge of God Almighty in a greater way?


By Shea Jubelirer

# Author Only SherAnne's Biography

SherAnne Shea Jubelirer has been doing writings ever since 1985, when she met Jeffrey David Jubelirer, a great poet, that's whenever she decided to do creative writing as a professional career.

She is a creative writer and poet. Sherry has been an author since back in 2000. Likewise, she has attended and was taking classes at 10 colleges and universities. She is now completing that's her 7th book called TO DO THAT'S LOVE WORKS.

Shea Jubelirer writes devotional poetry and spiritual memoirs and creative non-fiction.

She lives with her Author Only and Poet husband and dog named "Fixer" in Philadelphia, Pennsylvania.

SherAnne's books are available in Amazon, Barnes and Noble, and Books A Million.

# *Of Influences for Author Only, SherAnne Shea Jubelirer*

Of influences for and of this Author only, Writer and Poet are often family members, SherAnne's Father and mother and brothers and sister and Kelly's boys.

Likewise SherAnne was studying English Literature in graduate school.

All of the classic authors of this 20th century Were studied and read in class. Except they were mostly fiction authors with bits of truth and love written in such classic novels written by D.H. Lawrence, Virginia Woolf, James Joyce, and F. Scott Fitzgerald.

SherAnne believes PORTAIT Of AN ARTIST AS A YOUNG MAN is a great book. Virginia Woolf wrote of a room of one's own during the of the 20th century. And likewise, she wrote the great classic novel, MRS. DOLLOWAY. D. H. Lawrence wrote LADY CHATTERLY'S LOVER.

F. Scott Firzgerald wrote The Great Gatsby where Daisy's laughter sounded like money.

Likewise SherAnne's participation and coming to the Holy Catholic Churches of Philadelphia, sure was and is, for that has been more, wonderfully beautiful experiences thru the churches and priests who do ministry with the disciples. SherAnne was told she was for over doing that in life. Moreover and additionally, SherAnne was in religious life for a few years and we were studying prayers and comtemplations and mysticism.

# Fun Facts About Author Only, SherAnne Shea Jubelirer

We ever saw America as a family of friends and love ones during that's past 40 years of our life together.

My father was a very successful CEO of Pepperidge Farms

And second in command as a successful President of Campbell Soup Company.

SherAnne Marie Shea was born in Saint Cloud, Minnesota at Saint Mary's Hospital.

She is the firstborn of another six siblings who were called even together.

She was raised together with 1 sister and 4 brothers.

She loves coming to the Holy Catholic Churches of Philadelpia.

She now has 10 books on devotional poetry and spiritual memoirs and creative non-fiction.

She has had some mystical experiences as a religious, briefly and is now laity.

She was told she is a lay catholic mystic and visionary.

And working on her religious, holy faith and growing in graces is very important

For her salvation and peace.

# O Sweet, Holy Jesus, the Christ

Since every moment is thine O Sweet Holy Jesus,

I give praises to you, Sweet Holy Savior of that's mine.

Truly I do love you for

I am setting that was for all of us Shea's

And us Keifer's before you O Thee Sweet Holy Jesus

For You O God did promise wholesomeness

And soundness and that's love of pieces

For all have gone

And they will come again.

That we can truly live in some places

And love one another

As they were of love for and of full wellness of love.

I do already know the Truth was Jesus, the Christ.

God willing we do possess salvation and love

And we will be saved thru His Blessed, Holy and True Blood!

For Christ has died, Christ is risen

And Christ will come again!


By SherAnne Shea Jubelirer

# Day And Day Light

Thoughts of day and daylight flowing forth of truths.

Looking on a lighter side of everything of fine

And seeing we do belong to the Light of the World, Jesus, the Christ.

That's experiencing and thinking of and of thoughts of a new beginning again.

What will the Truth

And hope send our way?

Wishing for happiness

And making work can happen for us.

You do belong to me

And so does your great collection of poetry.

Make the words say and make us think

And spell for out there graces and God Almighty.

And I was looking and he was looking mighty graceful of that's past

For I do think we can create joy yet to be realized.


By Shea Jubelirer

# By Now

By now, I must make mention of this is truly like Amy Grant of whomever

That' s my father so favored her and her music, that I am now playing that.

Well, this is my father's world

And I was given to do anything to do before the books, that we were writing here.

Thee wonderful and great Poet, Jeffrey David Jubelirer has written 22 copy righted

Manuscripts and is perfecting and making all of that poetry and that matters, each

And every book and that's due for each and every book.

Of all that I can do this evening by writing this right here.

Honestly, I can do this now, and I am sure this went to the catholic churches likewise.

And as lonely

And by myself as I may be, I can be mighty good for salvation

And that's goals for heaven

For my folks that great couple where 2009 that's for sure were two greats to live on playing that.

And they were here at my place today.

I am full of gratitude

And gladness for my folks

And I am mighty good.

Do you, my dear readers believe my visions and dreams of whatsoever I do see of God Almighty for that's only one sure would hope so here.

And this is another book except I do keep doing writings without getting the typing done.

However that will come. I have done that's written of about over 14,000 pieces of writing already typed

And now I do have that's over 40 notebooks that do all need to be typed up.

And by now, I am writing more creative non-fiction to tell mostly of love

And truths and Jesus and of goodness and of beauty.

That then, of receiving Christ Jesus in holy communion is such that I must do.

Hope all is well,


Good night!


By SherAnne Shea Jubelirer

September 9, 2009

# *Of Signs And Wonders Of God Almighty*

Of wondering, I am sure we are doing just fine. And to find God Almighty in our life every day and to realize I do have Graces to seek Jesus and His Great and Holy Blood to be consistently applied on a daily basis and looking for more prayers, always. And of this anymore for now. That's a good look and for my books on accomplishing each and every day. We need love and I was reading that all we need is love so I do try to give love as I was only saying that's love forever. I do have to do God Almighty is here and He is always and everywhere. Let us revel and make remembrances of graces and loves. To do God will, yes he will.


By Shea Jubelirer

Printed by Libri Plureos GmbH in Hamburg, Germany